Keto Instant Omni Pro Air Fryer Oven Combo Cookbook

500-Day Crispy and Healthy Recipes for Low-Carb Ketogenic Diet to Burn Fat Fast | Fry, Bake, Grill & Roast Most Wanted Family Meals

Fsalia Crispo

Table of Contents

Introduction

Instant Omni Pro Air Fryer Oven Combo is so much more than just a healthy way to enjoy some crispy fried foods without worrying about getting fat. It is an appliance that can cook an incredible variety of dishes, including many that you probably never thought possible.

The recipes in this cookbook have been designed to give you a glimpse into the limitless potential of Instant Omni Pro Air Fryer Oven Combo on Keto diet. Once you see how simple and quickly it is to create healthy and delicious foods with this Oven, then your healthy and happy life begins. You can use it to enjoy flavorful low-fat, oil-free food every day.

The Instant Omni Pro Air Fryer Oven Combo is definitely for you. Especially Keto diet, it is aimed to lose weight diet without feeling hungry. With a low-carb, high-fat way of eating, it is remarkably effective at transforming people's lives, helping them shed pounds and find relief from common health conditions. Keto diet is a very popular that is embraced by many people due to its simple and delicious taste.

Chapter 1: Keto Diet Basics

What is Keto Diet?

The Keto diet is one of the most effective and popular diet plans comes with long term health benefits. Keto is a low-carb, high-fat diet plan that allows a moderate amount of protein during the diet period. Keto is not just a diet plan it completely changes your daily food eating habit towards natural and healthy food consumption. Generally, our body depends on glucose (carb) for energy to perform day-to-day activities. When the glucose level in our body increases the excess glucose is converted into glycogens and stored in liver and body cells.

The Keto diet is a low carb diet, so the carb consumption is reduced during a keto diet. Due to this glucose level is decreased and our body finds out the alternative source for energy. It breaks down fats for energy. This state of the body is also called ketosis. It is one of the metabolic processes where fats are broken down and produce ketones for energy. These ketones provide an endless source of energy to our body. The Keto diet is one of the most followed diets for weight loss purposes. It not only maintains your healthy body weight but also improves your physical and mental health.

How does Keto Diet Work?

In general, our body uses glucose (carb) as a primary source of energy. When we reduce the intake of carbohydrates during the diet, glucose level automatically reduces. In this condition, our body shifts itself to break down fats for energy in the absence of carbohydrates (glucose). In fat breaking process some fatty acids are released our livers convert these fatty acids into ketones.

Ketones are produced due to a chemical process when our body burns fat for energy instead of glucose. Most of the body organs and tissues use these ketones as an alternative source of energy. Ketones are one of the best fuels for our brain they fulfill more than 70% of our brain energy needs. The lack of glucose pushes our body into the state of ketosis.

How to Know Whether Your Body is in Ketosis or Not?

There are several sign and symptoms and methods which indicate that your body is in the state of ketosis or not. These signs, symptoms, and methods are mention as follows.

- **Increase in thirst and dry mouth**

This is one of the common side effects noticed when you are following a keto diet. In this state, your body loses excess sodium and water, so it is recommended that add 2 to 4 grams of sodium into your diet to balancing the electrolyte level into your body. This will also increase the urination process and increase thirst. These signs and symptoms indicate that your body is in a state of ketosis.

- **Keto Breath or Bad Breath**

This is one of the common side effects noticed during the first week of the keto diet. When your body breaks down fats for energy, in this process acetone are release and produce a fruity smell or nail polish remover like smell having the bad breath symptoms. This is happening due to keto diet plan adaptation. Keto breath or bad breath symptoms will indicate that your body is in the state of ketosis.

- **Rapid Weight Loss**

This happens when your body breaks down fats for energy instead of glucose (carb). If you notice that your weight is rapidly reduced during the first week of the keto diet, then. Rapid weight loss is another sign and symptom that indicates that your body is in the state of ketosis.

- **Blood Test**

A blood test is one of the common and accurate methods used to measure the ketones level. It is one of the few expensive methods of measuring blood ketones levels in diabetic patients. The blood test method is similar to a glucometer test. In this case, you need to use a keto meter instead of a glucometer with a lancet pen and test strips.

If the keto meter shows reading 0.5 and 3 mml/L which indicates that your body is in the state of ketosis.

- **Ketostix**

Ketostix is one of the accurate and inexpensive ways to check your ketones level in the urine. You just need to collect the urine in a clean urine container then dip the Ketostix and shake to remove the excess urine from the stick and wait for 15 seconds. After 15 minutes you have noticed that Ketostix color is changed. To measure the ketones level just follow the color guide match with your strip color to check the ketosis.

- **Increase focus and energy**

Most people notice that tiredness and sickness during the first few days of the keto diet. When your body uses ketones for energy. It not only improves your physical health but also improves your focus and energy. This is happening because 70% of brain energy needs are fulfilled by ketones. This is another sign which indicates that your body is in the state of ketosis.

The Advantages of Keto Diet

The keto diet is one of the most popular diets for years comes with various kinds of health benefits some of them are described as follows.

- **Rapid Weight loss**

If you are overweight and want to reduce the extra weight rapidly then the keto diet is one of the best choices to maintain your healthy body weight. During the keto diet, our body breaks down fats for energy instead of glucose. Due to this fat breaking process, you have notice rapid weight loss. The diet allows a moderate number of proteins, so you don't feel hungrier during the diet period. This will help to reduce your bodyweight rapidly and gives you long term weight loss benefits.

- **Improve your Brain Functions**

Keto diet is low carb diet, due to low carb consumption glucose level decreases and our body finds out alternative energy source by breaking the fats for energy. During the fat breaking process some chemical releases. Our liver converts these chemicals into ketones. To perform day-to-day operations our body use ketones as an energy source. It fulfills more than 70% of brain energy needs. Most of the study and research proves that ketones improve focus, attention and memory functions.

- **Effective on various medical conditions**

The keto diet is not only used for weight loss purposes but also used to treat various medical conditions like Alzheimer's, Parkinson's, type-2 diabetes, heart-related disease, blood pressure, and also in epilepsy conditions.

- **Improves Cholesterol Levels**

The keto diet is a low-carb high-fat diet. It allows you to consume healthy fats during the diet period. Healthy fats are responsible to improve the HDL (good cholesterol) level. Carbohydrates are one of the main reasons to increase the LDL (bad cholesterol) level. The Keto diet is a low-carb diet, so it decreases the LDL level and also reduces the risk of heart-related disease.

- **Control Appetite**

The keto diet is a low carb, high fat, and moderate protein diet. The diet is enriching with all essential nutrients the moderate protein in diet which helps prevent an increase in appetite. You never feel hungry after eating healthy keto diet food.

- **Longevity**

Keto diet is responsible to increase your lifespan. The keto diet allows you to consume healthy notorious and antioxidant-rich foods. This will help to cures various health-related problems that occur due to the consumption of unhealthy and poor diet. The scientific studies prove that the peoples who follow the keto diet can result in a significant drop in oxidative stress level. It also reduces the risk of diabetes, heart disease, and obesity and improves lifespan.

- Increase in energy levels

The keto diet shifts your body to breakdown fats for energy instead of glucose. During the fat breaking, process chemicals are released, and our liver converts it into ketones. Ketones provide energy to our body organ and tissues and long-lasting energy source to our body. Due to an increase in energy level, you feel active and fully energized the whole day.

Tips and Tricks for Successful Keto Journey

The following tips and tricks are helpful to complete your keto journey.

1. Limit Daily Carb Consumption

To stay in ketosis, it is recommended to consume 10 to 30 grams of carb daily. If you are an active person and doing hard exercise for 5 to 6 days a week then you can increase carb consumption. Don't eat too much carb it may build up glycogen storage.

2. Eat healthy fats

During the keto diet, it is recommended to eat healthy fats like avocado oil, olive oil, coconut oil, etc. avoid unhealthy fats like vegetable oil, sunflower oil, canola oil, etc. Healthy fat consumption will help to boost ketone levels in your body and keep your body in a ketosis state.

3. Get enough sleep

Due to Inadequate sleep, you feel hunger and it is one of the bad signs for your weight loss process. To stay in ketosis during the keto diet you need not only enough sleep but also get better quality sleep. Better quality means you should sleep in a cool and darkroom. The room temperature is maintained at 65 F and you need to sleep at least 7 hours a daily night to get complete enough sleep.

4. Consume Moderate Protein

In the keto diet our body breaks down fats for energy. In this fat breaking process some healthy muscles and fats. An adequate amount of protein consumption will help to repair this muscle and also maintain muscle mass. As per your body weight, it is recommended to consume 0.75 grams of protein per pound.

5. Regular exercise

Regular exercise during the keto diet will keep you energized throughout the day. It also increases the ketones level and decreases the carb from your body. Regular exercise keeps you fit and also maintains your blood sugar level.

6. Use MCT oils

Use coconut oil which contains healthy fats called MCT (Medium Chain Triglycerides). It is easily absorbed by the liver and converts into ketones. MCT oils provide an instant source of energy to our body and are converted into ketones. MCTs travel fast into your body and enter into your body cells without broken.

7. Stay Hydrated

When you follow the keto diet, it is important to keep your body hydrated. During the diet period, your body loses glycogens through the urination process. These glycogens hold 5 parts of water, so your body is dehydrated during the diet. To keep your body hydrated you need to consume smoothies, coffee, or tea during the diet period.

Chapter 2: Instant Omni Air Fryer Oven Combo Basics

Features of Instant Omni Air Fryer Oven Combo

As we know the Omni is a smart and multi-functional cooking appliance saves your kitchen countertop space by performing functions of the different appliance in a single one. These functions are pre-programmed so that you never worry about time and temperature settings. The front top display panel comes with these 9 smart functions and 2 cooking methods. These functions are

- **Air Fry:** This function is used to frying purpose, using this function you can fry a bowl of French fries within a tablespoon of oil. It makes your French fries crispy from outside and tender from inside.
- **Toast:** This function is used to toast your bread. You can put 6 slices of bread at a time into a middle rack your Instant Omni Air Fryer Oven Combo make it brown and crisp.
- **Bake:** You can use this to bake your favorite cake, cookies, brownies, muffins, and pizza. You can make a medium size (12 inches) pizza using this function.
- **Broil:** This function is used for browning the top portion of your desserts and casseroles. While using this function your oven produces dry heat from the top to cook your food.
- **Roast:** Roast function can be used to roast vegetables, meats, and your favorite foods. You can also roast a whole chicken at a time into Omni plus. In this function dry hot air covers your food from all sides to give you even cooking results.
- **Slow cook:** This function is used to cooks your food at low temperatures and also keeps your food warm. Due to lower temperature, it helps to preserve the nutritional values into your food.
- **Reheat:** Using this function you can reheat your leftover and frozen food it helps to crisp skin and retaining the moisture.

- **Proof:** During this function, halogen light is illuminated to keep your oven internal temperature warm it helps yeast for rising during the proofing process. It maintains 85° F to 95° F temperature during proof mode is on.
- **Dehydrate:** This function is used to dehydrate fruits and vegetables or meat slice for preserving. Making nuts and seed crispy, tempeh, crackers, oatmeal cookies, and drying your favorite fruits and vegetables.
- **Convect and Rotate:** These two are cooking methods. Convection and rotate are used to cook your favorite chicken with the help of rotisserie spit and forks.

How to Prepare a Meal in Omni Air Fryer Oven?

Cooking food into Omni is a faster and easy way to cook tasty and delicious food in a healthy cooking method. Following steps guides you to prepare fresh and healthy foods into your Instant Omni Air Fryer Oven Combo.

1. Prepare appliance by plug-in it into the power switch, the display light glows instantly then open the oven door and place crumb tray at the bottom notch of the oven. Always make sure that the oven is placed on a flat surface and leave at least 13 to 15 cm of space from all sides.
2. Choose the accessories as per the recipe needs and place them inside the oven at their correct position.
3. Preheat oven if needed, preheating oven saves your cooking time and also gives a nice texture to your food. Use your left side preset dial to select the appropriate program then adjust the time and temperature by using the right-side temp/time dial. You can also select cooking mode convection or rotate as per recipe requirements then finally press the start button. The preheating process is started the oven takes 4 to 5 minutes to get 400° F temperature.
4. After finishing the preheating process display indicates with a beep. Then insert the food into the oven and close the door. If you don't want to preheat the oven then just put your food into oven select cooking mode, adjust the desired time and temperature and press the start button to start the actual cooking process.

5. If the food requires turning or flipping then display indicates FLIP on screen. When you open the door to turn food than the current running program automatically paused. After closing the door, you need to press the start button to resume the cooking process.
6. At the end of the cooking process successfully the oven will beep and your food is ready to serve.

Cleaning and Maintenance

After every use, you must clean your Instant pot Instant Omni Air Fryer Oven Combo to keep it germ-free. After finishing the cooking some food particles are stuck into the wall of the Instant Omni Air Fryer Oven Combo. Just follow the following some simple steps to clean your Instant Omni Air Fryer Oven Combo.

1. Before starting the cleaning, process unplug your Omni oven from the socket. Open the oven door and cool it down completely at room temperature.
2. Then remove all the accessories like dripping pan, steel rack, air fryer basket, rotisseries, etc.
3. All the accessories used in Instant Omni Air Fryer Oven Combo are dishwasher safe. You can easily wash it into the dishwasher and after that dry it completely.
4. Now clean your oven from inside by using a clean and damp cloth. Carefully clean all inner walls using a damp cloth.
5. After finishing inner cleaning clean your oven exterior body with another clean and little damp cloth. Clean display and touch buttons carefully with a soft cloth.
6. Now assemble all the removable parts like steel rack, dripping pan, and other accessories to its original position.
7. Check the power cable for any damage if it is damaged then change it in the authorized service center. If the power cable is ok then clean the cable with a dry cloth.

Now your instant pot Instant Omni Air Fryer Oven Combo is ready for next use.

Chapter 3: Breakfast Recipes

Moist Lemon Poppy Seed Muffins

Preparation Time: 5 minutes

Cooking Time: 20 minutes

Serve: 12

Ingredients:

- 3 tbsp poppy seeds
- 1/4 tsp baking soda
- 10 tbsp maple syrup
- 2 tbsp lemon zest
- 6 tbsp lemon juice
- 4/5 cup almond milk
- 1/4 cup coconut oil, melted
- 2 tsp baking powder
- 1 1/4 cups flour
- 1 1/4 cups almond meal
- 1 tsp vanilla
- Pinch of salt

Directions:

1. Line muffin tray with cupcake liners and set aside.
2. In a large bowl, mix together oil, milk, lemon zest, vanilla, lemon juice, poppy seeds, maple syrup, and almond meal.
3. Add flour, baking soda, and baking powder. Stir until well combined.
4. Pour batter into the prepared muffin tray
5. Select bake mode and set the omni to 350 F for 20 minutes once the oven beeps, place muffin tray into the oven.
6. Serve and enjoy.

Nutritional Value (Amount per Serving):

- Calories 240
- Fat 14.5 g
- Carbohydrates 25.5 g
- Sugar 11.5 g
- Protein 4.3 g
- Cholesterol 0 mg

Crustless Quiche

Preparation Time: 5 minutes

Cooking Time: 45 minutes

Serve: 6

Ingredients:

- 6 eggs
- 1 cup cheddar cheese, grated
- 1 cup tomatoes, chopped
- 1 cup milk
- Pepper
- Salt

Directions:

1. Spray an 8-inch pie dish with cooking spray and set aside.
2. In a bowl, whisk eggs with cheese, milk, pepper, and salt. Add tomatoes and stir well.
3. Pour egg mixture into the prepared pie dish.
4. Select bake mode and set the omni to 350 F for 45 minutes once the oven beeps, place the pie dish into the oven.
5. Serve and enjoy.

Nutritional Value (Amount per Serving):

- Calories 165
- Fat 11.5 g
- Carbohydrates 3.8 g
- Sugar 3.1 g
- Protein 11.8 g
- Cholesterol 187 mg

Cinnamon Pumpkin Bread

Preparation Time: 5 minutes

Cooking Time: 50 minutes

Serve: 12

Ingredients:

- 2 eggs
- 2 cups flour
- 1 cup can pumpkin puree
- 1/2 cup milk
- 2/3 cup olive oil
- 1/4 tsp ground cloves
- 1/2 tsp ground allspice
- 1/2 tsp ground cinnamon
- 2 tsp baking powder
- 1 cup of sugar

Directions:

1. Spray a 9-inch loaf pan with cooking spray.
2. In a bowl, whisk together flour, sugar, baking powder, cinnamon, allspice, and cloves.
3. In a large bowl, whisk together eggs, oil, and pumpkin puree.
4. Add dry ingredients mixture into the wet mixture and mix until well combined.
5. Pour batter into the prepared loaf pan.
6. Select bake mode and set the omni to 375 F for 50 minutes once the oven beeps, place loaf pan into the oven.
7. Slice and serve.

Nutritional Value (Amount per Serving):

- Calories 255
- Fat 12.4 g
- Carbohydrates 34.5 g
- Sugar 17.6 g
- Protein 3.5 g
- Cholesterol 28 mg

Breakfast Kale Muffins

Preparation Time: 5 minutes

Cooking Time: 30 minutes

Serve: 8

Ingredients:

- 6 eggs
- 1 cup kale, chopped
- 1/2 cup milk
- 1/4 cup chives, chopped
- Pepper & salt, to taste

Directions:

1. Spray muffin pan with cooking spray and set aside.
2. Add all ingredients into the mixing bowl and whisk well.
3. Pour mixture into the prepared muffin pan.
4. Select bake mode and set the omni to 350 F for 30 minutes once the oven beeps, place muffin pan into the oven.
5. Serve and enjoy.

Nutritional Value (Amount per Serving):

- Calories 59
- Fat 3.6 g
- Carbohydrates 2 g
- Sugar 1 g
- Protein 5 g
- Cholesterol 124 mg

Simple Cinnamon Baked Oatmeal

Preparation Time: 5 minutes

Cooking Time: 25 minutes

Serve: 6

Ingredients:

- 2 eggs, lightly beaten
- 1 1/4 cup milk
- 1/2 cup butter, melted
- 1 cup brown sugar
- 3 cups quick oats
- 1 tsp ground cinnamon
- 1 tsp vanilla
- 1 tbsp baking powder

Directions:

1. Spray an 8-inch baking dish with cooking spray.
2. In a bowl, whisk sugar, vanilla, cinnamon, baking powder, eggs, milk, and butter until well combined. Add oats and stir well.
3. Pour oat mixture into the prepared baking dish.
4. Select bake mode and set the omni to 350 F for 25 minutes once the oven beeps, place the baking dish into the oven.
5. Serve and enjoy.

Nutritional Value (Amount per Serving):

- Calories 434
- Fat 20.5 g
- Carbohydrates 55.6 g
- Sugar 26.4 g
- Protein 9.1 g
- Cholesterol 99 mg

Berry Oatmeal

Preparation Time: 5 minutes

Cooking Time: 20 minutes

Serve: 4

Ingredients:

- 1 egg
- 1/4 cup maple syrup
- 1 1/2 cups milk
- 1 1/2 tsp baking powder
- 2 cups old fashioned oats
- 1 cup blueberries
- 1/2 cup blackberries
- 1/2 cup strawberries, sliced
- 1/2 tsp salt

Directions:

1. Grease baking dish and set aside.
2. In a mixing bowl, mix together oats, salt, and baking powder.
3. Add vanilla, egg, maple syrup, and milk and stir well.
4. Add berries and stir well.
5. Pour mixture into the baking dish.
6. Select bake mode and set the omni to 375 F for 20 minutes once the oven beeps, place the baking dish into the oven.
7. Serve and enjoy.

Nutritional Value (Amount per Serving):

- Calories 461
- Fat 8.4 g
- Carbohydrates 80.7 g
- Sugar 23.4 g
- Protein 15 g
- Cholesterol 48 mg

Easy Broccoli Egg Bake

Preparation Time: 5 minutes

Cooking Time: 30 minutes

Serve: 12

Ingredients:

- 12 eggs
- 1 onion, diced
- 1 cup milk
- 1 1/2 cups cheddar cheese, shredded
- 2 cups broccoli florets, chopped
- Pepper & salt, to taste

Directions:

1. Grease a 9*13-inch baking dish and set aside.
2. In a large bowl, whisk eggs with milk, pepper, and salt. Add cheese, broccoli, and onion and stir well.
3. Pour egg mixture into the prepared baking dish.
4. Select bake mode and set the omni to 390 F for 30 minutes once the oven beeps, place the baking dish into the oven.
5. Serve and enjoy.

Nutritional Value (Amount per Serving):

- Calories 139
- Fat 9.5 g
- Carbohydrates 3.4 g
- Sugar 2 g
- Protein 10.3 g
- Cholesterol 180 mg

Italian Breakfast Frittata

Preparation Time: 5 minutes

Cooking Time: 30 minutes

Serve: 4

Ingredients:

- 8 eggs
- 2 zucchini, chopped and cooked
- 1 tbsp fresh parsley, chopped
- 3 tbsps parmesan cheese, grated
- Pepper & salt, to taste

Directions:

1. Grease baking dish and set aside.
2. In a mixing bowl, whisk eggs with pepper and salt.
3. Add parsley, cheese, and zucchini and stir well.
4. Pour egg mixture into the prepared baking dish.
5. Select bake mode and set the omni to 350 F for 30 minutes once the oven beeps, place the baking dish into the oven.
6. Serve and enjoy.

Nutritional Value (Amount per Serving):

- Calories 176
- Fat 11.2 g
- Carbohydrates 4.4 g
- Sugar 2.4 g
- Protein 15.7 g
- Cholesterol 335 mg

Mini Egg Muffins

Preparation Time: 5 minutes

Cooking Time: 20 minutes

Serve: 9

Ingredients:

- 4 eggs
- 1/4 cup Sun-dried tomatoes, chopped
- 1/2 cup Kale, chopped
- ½ cup egg whites
- Pepper & salt, to taste

Directions:

1. Spray muffin pan with cooking spray and set aside.
2. In a mixing bowl, whisk eggs and egg whites.
3. Add sun-dried tomatoes, kale, pepper, and salt and whisk well.
4. Pour egg mixture into the prepared muffin pan
5. Select bake mode and set the omni to 350 F for 20 minutes once the oven beeps, place muffin pan into the oven.
6. Serve and enjoy.

Nutritional Value (Amount per Serving):

- Calories 49
- Fat 2.1 g
- Carbohydrates 3.5 g
- Sugar 0.5 g
- Protein 4.3 g
- Cholesterol 73 mg

Oatmeal Cake

Preparation Time: 5 minutes

Cooking Time: 25 minutes

Serve: 8

Ingredients:

- 2 eggs
- 1 cup oats
- 1 apple, peeled & chopped
- 1 tbsp butter
- 3 tbsp yogurt
- 1/2 tsp baking powder
- 1/2 tsp baking soda
- 1 tsp cinnamon
- 1 tsp vanilla
- 3 tbsps honey

Directions:

1. Add 3/4 cup oats and remaining ingredients into the blender and blend until smooth.
2. Add remaining oats and mix well.
3. Pour batter into the parchment-lined baking pan.
4. Select bake mode and set the omni to 350 F for 25 minutes once the oven beeps, place baking pan into the oven.
5. Slice and serve.

Nutritional Value (Amount per Serving):

- Calories 112
- Fat 3.3 g
- Carbohydrates 18.2 g
- Sugar 10 g
- Protein 3.2 g
- Cholesterol 45 mg

Chapter 4: Poultry Recipes

Delicious Chicken Tenders

Preparation Time: 5 minutes

Cooking Time: 20 minutes

Serve: 4

Ingredients:

- 1 lbs chicken tenders
- 1 garlic clove, minced
- 1/2 oz fresh lemon juice
- 2 tbsp fresh tarragon, chopped
- 1/2 cup whole grain mustard
- 1/2 tsp paprika
- 1/2 tsp pepper
- 1/4 tsp kosher salt

Directions:

1. Add all ingredients except chicken to the large bowl and mix well.
2. Add chicken to the bowl and stir until well coated.
3. Place chicken on a baking dish and cover dish with foil.
4. Select bake mode and set the omni to 425 F for 20 minutes once the oven beeps, place the baking dish into the oven.
5. Serve and enjoy.

Nutritional Value (Amount per Serving):

- Calories 242
- Fat 9.5 g
- Carbohydrates 3.1 g
- Sugar 0.1 g
- Protein 33.2 g
- Cholesterol 101 mg

Juicy Spicy Chicken Wings

Preparation Time: 5 minutes

Cooking Time: 25 minutes

Serve: 4

Ingredients:

- 2 lbs chicken wings
- 1/2 tsp Worcestershire sauce
- 1/2 tsp Tabasco
- 6 tbsp butter, melted
- 12 oz hot sauce

Directions:

1. Spray air fryer basket with cooking spray.
2. Add chicken wings into the air fryer basket.
3. Place air fryer basket into the oven and select air fry mode set omni to the 380 F for 25 minutes. Stir twice.
4. Meanwhile, in a bowl, mix together hot sauce, Worcestershire sauce, and butter. Set aside.
5. Add cooked chicken wings into the sauce bowl and toss well.
6. Serve and enjoy.

Nutritional Value (Amount per Serving):

- Calories 594
- Fat 34.4 g
- Carbohydrates 1.6 g
- Sugar 1.2 g
- Protein 66.2 g
- Cholesterol 248 mg

Caribbean Chicken

Preparation Time: 5 minutes

Cooking Time: 10 minutes

Serve: 8

Ingredients:

- 3 lbs chicken thigh, skinless and boneless
- 1 tbsp cayenne
- 1 tbsp cinnamon
- 1 tbsp coriander powder
- 3 tbsp coconut oil, melted
- 1/2 tsp ground nutmeg
- 1/2 tsp ground ginger
- Pepper
- Salt

Directions:

1. In a small bowl, mix together all ingredients except chicken.
2. Rub bowl mixture all over the chicken.
3. Spray air fryer basket with cooking spray.
4. Place chicken into the air fryer basket.
5. Place air fryer basket into the oven and select air fry mode set omni to the 390 F for 10 minutes.
6. Serve and enjoy.

Nutritional Value (Amount per Serving):

- Calories 373
- Fat 17.9 g
- Carbohydrates 1.2 g
- Sugar 0.1 g
- Protein 49.3 g
- Cholesterol 151 mg

Delicious Turkey Breast

Preparation Time: 5 minutes

Cooking Time: 45 minutes

Serve: 4

Ingredients:

- 1 lb turkey breast, cut into 1-inch cubes
- 1 tsp garlic powder
- 1/2 lb Brussels sprouts, cut in half
- 2 tbsp olive oil
- 1 cup mushrooms, cleaned
- Pepper
- Salt

Directions:

1. In a small bowl, mix oil, garlic powder, pepper, and salt.
2. In a baking dish, mix together turkey, mushrooms, and Brussels sprouts. Pour oil mixture on top.
3. Cover dish with foil. Select bake mode and set the omni to 350 F for 45 minutes once the oven beeps, place the baking dish into the oven.
4. Serve and enjoy.

Nutritional Value (Amount per Serving):

- Calories 209
- Fat 9.1 g
- Carbohydrates 11 g
- Sugar 5.7 g
- Protein 22 g
- Cholesterol 49 mg

Chicken Fajita Casserole

Preparation Time: 5 minutes

Cooking Time: 30 minutes

Serve: 4

Ingredients:

- 1 lb cooked chicken, shredded
- 7 oz shredded cheese
- 2 tbsp tex-mex seasoning
- 1 onion, sliced
- 1 bell pepper, sliced
- 1/3 cup mayonnaise
- 7 oz cream cheese
- Pepper
- Salt

Directions:

1. Spray a baking dish with butter and set aside.
2. Mix all ingredients except 2 oz shredded cheese in a prepared baking dish.
3. Spread remaining cheese on top.
4. Select bake mode and set the omni to 400 F for 15 minutes once the oven beeps, place the baking dish into the oven.
5. Serve and enjoy.

Nutritional Value (Amount per Serving):

- Calories 641
- Fat 43.8 g
- Carbohydrates 11.5 g
- Sugar 4.3 g
- Protein 49.7 g
- Cholesterol 199 mg

Chicken with Olives

Preparation Time: 5 minutes

Cooking Time: 35 minutes

Serve: 4

Ingredients:

- 1 lb chicken breasts, skinless, boneless and cut into pieces
- 1/3 cup vinaigrette dressing
- 1 medium onion, diced
- 3 cups potatoes cut into pieces
- 4 cups Brussels sprouts, trimmed and quartered
- 1/4 cup olives, quartered
- 1 tsp oregano
- 1 1/2 tsp Dijon mustard
- 1 lemon juice
- 1/4 tsp pepper
- 1/4 tsp salt

Directions:

1. Place chicken in the center of cooking pan then place potatoes, sprouts, and onions around the chicken.
2. In a small bowl, mix together vinaigrette, oregano, mustard, lemon juice, and salt and pour over chicken and veggies. Sprinkle olives and season with pepper.
3. Select bake mode and set the omni to 400 F for 20 minutes once the oven beeps, place the cooking pan into the oven.
4. Transfer chicken to a plate. Stir the vegetables and roast for 15 minutes more.
5. Serve and enjoy.

Nutritional Value (Amount per Serving):

- Calories 397
- Fat 13 g
- Carbohydrates 31.4 g
- Sugar 6.7 g
- Protein 38.3 g
- Cholesterol 101 mg

Tasty Chicken Tandoori

Preparation Time: 5 minutes

Cooking Time: 15 minutes

Serve: 4

Ingredients:

- 1 lb chicken tenders, cut in half
- 1 tsp paprika
- 1 tbsp garlic, minced
- 1 tbsp ginger, minced
- 1/4 cup yogurt
- 1 tsp garam masala
- 1 tsp turmeric
- 1 tsp cayenne pepper
- 1/4 cup parsley, chopped
- 1 tsp salt

Directions:

1. Add all ingredients into the large bowl and mix well. Place in refrigerator for 30 minutes.
2. Spray air fryer basket with cooking spray.
3. Add marinated chicken into the preheated air fryer basket.
4. Place air fryer basket into the oven and select air fry mode set omni to the 350 F for 15 minutes. Turn chicken after 10 minutes.
5. Serve and enjoy.

Nutritional Value (Amount per Serving):

- Calories 240
- Fat 8.9 g
- Carbohydrates 3.9 g
- Sugar 1.3 g
- Protein 34.2 g
- Cholesterol 102 mg

Delicious Fajita Chicken

Preparation Time: 5 minutes

Cooking Time: 15 minutes

Serve: 4

Ingredients:

- 4 chicken breasts, make horizontal cuts on each piece
- 1 bell pepper, sliced
- 2 tbsp fajita seasoning
- 1/2 cup cheddar cheese, shredded
- 1 onion, sliced
- 2 tbsp olive oil

Directions:

1. Rub oil and seasoning all over the chicken breast.
2. Place chicken into the air fryer basket and top with bell peppers and onion.
3. Place air fryer basket into the oven and select air fry mode set omni to the 380 F for 15 minutes.
4. Remove chicken and veggies from air fryer and place on foil piece.
5. Top with shredded cheese and serve.

Nutritional Value (Amount per Serving):

- Calories 419
- Fat 22.2 g
- Carbohydrates 8.2 g
- Sugar 2.7 g
- Protein 44.6 g
- Cholesterol 139 mg

Mustard Chicken Tenders

Preparation Time: 5 minutes

Cooking Time: 12 minutes

Serve: 4

Ingredients:

- 1 lb chicken tenders
- 1 egg, lightly beaten
- 1/2 tsp paprika
- 1 cup pecans, crushed
- 1/4 cup ground mustard
- 1 tsp pepper
- 1 tsp salt

Directions

1. Spray air fryer basket with cooking spray.
2. Add chicken into the large bowl. Season with paprika, pepper, and salt. Add mustard mix well.
3. In another bowl, add egg and whisk well.
4. In a shallow dish, add crushed pecans.
5. Dip chicken into the egg then coats with crushed pecans. Place into the air fryer basket.
6. Place air fryer basket into the oven and select air fry mode set omni to the 350 F for 12 minutes.
7. Serve and enjoy.

Nutritional Value (Amount per Serving):

- Calories 454
- Fat 30.3 g
- Carbohydrates 7.6 g
- Sugar 1.7 g
- Protein 39.4 g
- Cholesterol 142 mg

Easy Turkey Meatballs

Preparation Time: 5 minutes

Cooking Time: 12 minutes

Serve: 4

Ingredients:

- 1 egg
- 2 tbsp coconut flour
- 1 lb ground turkey
- 1 garlic clove, minced
- 2 green onion, chopped
- 1/4 cup celery, chopped
- 1/4 cup carrots, grated
- Pepper
- Salt

Directions:

1. Spray air fryer basket with cooking spray.
2. Add all ingredients into the large bowl and mix until well combined.
3. Make small balls from the meat mixture and place it into the air fryer basket.
4. Place air fryer basket into the oven and select air fry mode set omni to the 400 F for 12 minutes. Turn halfway through.
5. Serve and enjoy.

Nutritional Value (Amount per Serving):

- Calories 274
- Fat 14.3 g
- Carbohydrates 6.8 g
- Sugar 0.7 g
- Protein 33.7 g
- Cholesterol 157 mg

Chapter 5: Vegetarian Recipes

Baked Zucchini Eggplant

Preparation Time: 5 minutes

Cooking Time: 35 minutes

Serve: 6

Ingredients:

- 3 medium zucchini, sliced
- 1 medium eggplant, sliced
- 1 tbsp olive oil
- 4 garlic cloves, minced
- 1/4 tsp pepper
- 3 oz parmesan cheese, grated
- 1/4 cup parsley, chopped
- 1/4 cup basil, chopped
- 1 cup cherry tomatoes, halved
- 1/4 tsp salt

Directions:

1. Spray baking dish with cooking spray.
2. In a bowl, add cherry tomatoes, eggplant, zucchini, olive oil, garlic, cheese, basil, pepper, and salt toss well until combined.
3. Transfer eggplant mixture into the baking dish.
4. Select bake mode and set the omni to 350 F for 35 minutes once the oven beeps, place the baking dish into the oven.
5. Garnish with parsley and serve.

Nutritional Value (Amount per Serving):

- Calories 110
- Fat 5.8 g
- Carbohydrates 10.4 g
- Sugar 4.8 g
- Protein 7 g
- Cholesterol 10 mg

Zucchini Egg Bake

Preparation Time: 5 minutes

Cooking Time: 30 minutes

Serve: 4

Ingredients:

- 6 eggs
- 1/2 tsp dill
- 1/2 tsp oregano
- 1/2 tsp basil
- 1/2 tsp baking powder
- 1/2 cup almond flour
- 1 cup cheddar cheese, shredded
- 1 cup kale, chopped
- 1 onion, chopped
- 1 cup zucchini, shredded and squeezed out all liquid
- 1/2 cup milk
- 1/4 tsp salt

Directions:

1. Grease 9*9-inch baking dish and set aside.
2. In a large bowl, whisk eggs with milk.
3. Add remaining ingredients and stir until well combined.
4. Pour egg mixture into the prepared baking dish.
5. Select bake mode and set the omni to 375 F for 30 minutes once the oven beeps, place the baking dish into the oven.
6. Serve and enjoy.

Nutritional Value (Amount per Serving):

- Calories 269
- Fat 18.4 g
- Carbohydrates 8.9 g
- Sugar 3.8 g
- Protein 18.3 g
- Cholesterol 278 mg

Mac & Cheese

Preparation Time: 5 minutes

Cooking Time: 20 minutes

Serve: 10

Ingredients:

- 1 lb cooked macaroni
- 1/2 cup flour
- 1/2 cup butter
- 1/2 cup breadcrumbs
- 12 oz cheddar cheese, shredded
- 4 1/2 cups unsweetened almond milk
- Pepper
- Salt

Directions:

1. Melt butter in a pan over medium heat.
2. Remove pan from heat and slowly add flour, salt, and pepper in melted butter.
3. Add ½ cup milk and stir until well blended.
4. Return to heat and slowly add remaining milk.
5. Add cheese and stir until cheese is melted.
6. Pour over cooked macaroni and stir well.
7. Transfer macaroni in a casserole dish and sprinkle with breadcrumbs.
8. Place casserole dish in Instant Omni Air Fryer Oven Combo Bakes at 350 F for 15-20 minutes.
9. Serve and enjoy.

Nutritional Value (Amount per Serving):

- Calories 449
- Fat 23.1 g
- Carbohydrates 43.9 g
- Sugar 1.8 g
- Protein 16.3 g
- Cholesterol 60 mg

Delicious Potato Patties

Preparation Time: 10 minutes

Cooking Time: 8 minutes

Serve: 2

Ingredients:

- 1 egg, beaten
- 1/4 tsp onion powder
- 1/4 tsp garlic powder
- 1 cup mashed potatoes
- 2 tbsp green onion, chopped
- 1 cup breadcrumbs
- 1/2 cup flour
- 1/2 cup cheddar cheese, shredded
- Pepper
- Salt

Directions:

1. Spray cooking pan with cooking spray and set aside.
2. In a bowl, mix together mashed potatoes, green onion, cheese, onion powder, and garlic powder.
3. Add flour, egg, and breadcrumbs in three separate bowls.
4. Make patties from potato mixture then roll in flour, dip in eggs, and coat with breadcrumbs.
5. Place patties on a cooking pan.
6. Place cooking pan into the oven and select air fry mode set omni to the 370 F for 8 minutes.
7. Serve and enjoy.

Nutritional Value (Amount per Serving):

- Calories 577
- Fat 16.2 g
- Carbohydrates 83.8 g
- Sugar 4.1 g
- Protein 23.3 g
- Cholesterol 114 mg

Roasted Broccoli Cauliflower

Preparation Time: 5 minutes

Cooking Time: 15 minutes

Serve: 12

Ingredients:

- 4 cups broccoli florets
- 2/3 cup parmesan cheese, grated and divided
- 4 cups cauliflower florets
- 6 garlic cloves, minced
- 1/3 cup olive oil
- Pepper
- Salt

Directions:

1. Preheat the oven to 400 F.
2. Spray a baking dish with cooking spray and set aside.
3. Add cauliflower, broccoli, half cheese, garlic, and olive oil in a bowl and toss well. Season with pepper and salt.
4. Arrange broccoli and cauliflower mixture on a prepared baking dish.
5. Select bake mode and set the omni to 400 F for 15 minutes once the oven beeps, place the baking dish into the oven.
6. Just before serving add remaining cheese and toss well.
7. Serve and enjoy.

Nutritional Value (Amount per Serving):

- Calories 86
- Fat 6.9 g
- Carbohydrates 4.5 g
- Sugar 1.3 g
- Protein 3.4 g
- Cholesterol 4 mg

Roasted Apple Sweet Potatoes

Preparation Time: 5 minutes

Cooking Time: 30 minutes

Serve: 2

Ingredients:

- 2 large sweet potatoes, diced
- 2 tsp cinnamon
- 2 large green apples, diced
- 2 tbsp maple syrup
- 1 tbsp olive oil

Directions:

1. In a large bowl, add sweet potatoes, oil, cinnamon, and apples and toss well.
2. Spread sweet potatoes mixture onto the cooking pan.
3. Select bake mode and set the omni to 400 F for 30 minutes once the oven beeps, place the cooking pan into the oven.
4. Drizzle with maple syrup and serve.

Nutritional Value (Amount per Serving):

- Calories 352
- Fat 7.6 g
- Carbohydrates 74 g
- Sugar 35.7 g
- Protein 2.2 g
- Cholesterol 0 mg

Baked Vegetables

Preparation Time: 5 minutes

Cooking Time: 20 minutes

Serve: 4

Ingredients:

- 4 bell peppers
- 2 cups mushrooms
- 1/4 tsp black pepper
- 2 tbsp olive oil
- 2 eggplants
- 1 tsp salt

Directions:

1. Cut all vegetables into the small bite-sized pieces and place in a baking dish.
2. Drizzle vegetables with olive oil and season with pepper and salt.
3. Select bake mode and set the omni to 390 F for 20 minutes once the oven beeps, place the baking dish into the oven.
4. Serve and enjoy.

Nutritional Value (Amount per Serving):

- Calories 174
- Fat 7.9 g
- Carbohydrates 26.3 g
- Sugar 14.8 g
- Protein 5 g
- Cholesterol 0 mg

Parmesan Hassel back Potatoes

Preparation Time: 10 minutes

Cooking Time: 40 minutes

Serve: 2

Ingredients:

- 2 potatoes, make the thin slices
- 2 tbsp butter, melted
- 3 tbsp mushrooms, sliced
- 4 tbsp parmesan cheese, grated
- Pepper
- Salt

Directions:

1. Spray the cooking pan with cooking spray and set aside.
2. Slide mushroom slices into each slit.
3. Place potatoes on cooking pan and brush with half-melted butter.
4. Place cooking pan into the oven and select air fry mode set omni to the 350 F for 20 minutes.
5. Turn potatoes to the other side and brush with remaining butter and air fry for 20 minutes more.
6. Sprinkle with parmesan cheese and serve.

Nutritional Value (Amount per Serving):

- Calories 345
- Fat 18 g
- Carbohydrates 34.8 g
- Sugar 2.6 g
- Protein 13.4 g
- Cholesterol 51 mg

Baked Egg Tomato

Preparation Time: 5 minutes

Cooking Time: 30 minutes

Serve: 2

Ingredients:

- 2 eggs
- 1 tsp fresh parsley
- 2 large fresh tomatoes
- Pepper
- Salt

Directions:

1. Cut the top of the tomato and spoon out the tomato innards.
2. Break the egg in each tomato. Place tomatoes on the cooking pan.
3. Select bake mode and set the omni to 350 F for 30 minutes once the oven beeps, place the cooking pan into the oven.
4. Season with pepper, and salt.
5. Garnish with parsley and serve.

Nutritional Value (Amount per Serving):

- Calories 96
- Fat 4.7 g
- Carbohydrates 7.5 g
- Sugar 5.1 g
- Protein 7.2 g
- Cholesterol 164 mg

Tasty Potato Fries

Preparation Time: 10 minutes

Cooking Time: 20 minutes

Serve: 2

Ingredients:

- 1 lb potatoes, wash, peel and cut into fries shape
- 1/4 tsp chili powder
- 1/2 tbsp olive oil
- 1/4 tsp smoked paprika
- Salt

Directions:

1. Spray air fryer basket with cooking spray.
2. Add potato fries in a large bowl and drizzle with olive oil. Season with paprika, chili powder, and salt.
3. Add potato fries into the air fryer basket.
4. Place air fryer basket into the oven and select air fry mode set omni to the 370 F for 20 minutes. Stir twice.
5. Serve and enjoy.

Nutritional Value (Amount per Serving):

- Calories 188
- Fat 3.8 g
- Carbohydrates 36 g
- Sugar 2.7 g
- Protein 3.9 g
- Cholesterol 0 mg

Chapter 6: Meat Recipes

Cheese Stuffed Pork Chops

Preparation Time: 10 minutes

Cooking Time: 35 minutes

Serve: 4

Ingredients:

- 4 pork chops, boneless and thick-cut
- 2 tbsp olives, chopped
- 2 tbsp sun-dried tomatoes, chopped
- 1/2 cup feta cheese, crumbled
- 3 garlic cloves, minced
- 2 tbsp fresh parsley, chopped

Directions:

1. In a bowl, combine together feta cheese, garlic, parsley, olives, and sun-dried tomatoes.
2. Stuff cheese mixture into each pork chops. Season pork chops with pepper and salt.
3. Place stuffed pork chops on cooking pan.
4. Select bake mode and set the omni to 375 F for 35 minutes once the oven beeps, place the cooking pan into the oven.
5. Serve and enjoy.

Nutritional Value (Amount per Serving):

- Calories 315
- Fat 24.4 g
- Carbohydrates 2.1 g
- Sugar 1 g
- Protein 20.9 g
- Cholesterol 85 mg

Artichoke Pepper Beef

Preparation Time: 10 minutes

Cooking Time: 6 hours

Serve: 6

Ingredients:

- 2 lbs stew beef, cut into 1-inch cubes
- 12 oz roasted red peppers, drained and sliced
- 12 oz artichoke hearts, drained
- 1 onion, diced
- 2 cups marinara sauce
- 1 tsp dried basil
- 1 tsp dried oregano

Directions:

1. Add all ingredients into the Dutch oven and stir well to combine.
2. Cover and place in Instant Omni Air Fryer Oven Combo.
3. Select slow cook mode and set the omni to low for 6 hours. Press start.
4. Serve and enjoy.

Nutritional Value (Amount per Serving):

- Calories 343
- Fat 11.6 g
- Carbohydrates 22.8 g
- Sugar 11.2 g
- Protein 37.3 g
- Cholesterol 2 mg

Easy Pork Tenderloin

Preparation Time: 10 minutes

Cooking Time: 35 minutes

Serve: 6

Ingredients:

- 2 lbs pork tenderloin
- 2 garlic cloves, chopped
- Pepper
- Salt

For the spice mix:

- 1/2 tsp allspice
- 1 tsp cinnamon
- 1 tsp cumin
- 1 tsp coriander
- 1/4 tsp cayenne
- 1 tsp oregano
- 1/4 tsp cloves

Directions:

1. In a small bowl, mix together all spice ingredients and set aside.
2. Using a sharp knife make slits on pork tenderloin and insert garlic into each slit.
3. Rub spice mixture over pork tenderloin. Sprinkle with pepper and salt.
4. Spray cooking pan with cooking spray.
5. Place pork tenderloin on cooking pan.
6. Select bake mode and set the omni to 375 F for 35 minutes once the oven beeps, place the cooking pan into the oven.
7. Slice and serve.

Nutritional Value (Amount per Serving):

- Calories 222
- Fat 5.5 g
- Carbohydrates 1.2 g
- Sugar 0.1 g
- Protein 39.8 g
- Cholesterol 110 mg

Quick & Easy Kabab

Preparation Time: 10 minutes

Cooking Time: 10 minutes

Serve: 4

Ingredients:

- 1 lb ground beef
- 1/4 cup fresh parsley, chopped
- 1 tbsp vegetable oil
- 2 tbsp kabab spice mix
- 1 tbsp garlic, minced
- 1 tsp salt

Directions:

1. Add all ingredients into the mixing bowl and mix until well combined. Place in refrigerator for 30 minutes.
2. Divide mixture into the four equal portions and make sausage shape kabab.
3. Spray air fryer basket with cooking spray.
4. Place kabab into the air fryer basket.
5. Place air fryer basket into the oven and select air fry mode set omni to the 370 F for 10 minutes.
6. Serve and enjoy.

Nutritional Value (Amount per Serving):

- Calories 255
- Fat 10.7 g
- Carbohydrates 2 g
- Sugar 0.2 g
- Protein 35.1 g
- Cholesterol 101 mg

Garlic Pork Sirloin Roast

Preparation Time: 10 minutes

Cooking Time: 1 hour 15 minutes

Serve: 4

Ingredients:

- 2 lbs pork sirloin roast
- 2 tbsp olive oil
- 4 garlic cloves, sliced
- 1/2 tsp pepper
- 1 tsp salt

Directions:

1. Using a sharp knife make slits on top of roast and stuff sliced garlic in each slit. Season pork roast with pepper and salt.
2. Heat olive oil in a pan over medium-high heat.
3. Place roast on the hot pan and cook until brown from all the sides.
4. Transfer pork roast on a cooking pan.
5. Select bake mode and set the omni to 350 F for 60-70 minutes once the oven beeps, place cooking pan into the oven. Turn roast halfway through.
6. Slice and serve.

Nutritional Value (Amount per Serving):

- Calories 535
- Fat 28.4 g
- Carbohydrates 1.2 g
- Sugar 0 g
- Protein 64.9 g
- Cholesterol 195 mg

Oregano Lamb Chops

Preparation Time: 10 minutes

Cooking Time: 5 minutes

Serve: 2

Ingredients:

- 4 lamb chops
- 1 garlic clove, minced
- 1/2 tbsp fresh oregano, chopped
- 1 1/2 tbsp olive oil
- Pepper
- Salt

Directions:

1. Mix together garlic, olive oil, oregano, pepper, and salt and rub over lamb chops.
2. Place lamb chops on the cooking pan.
3. Place cooking pan into the oven and select air fry mode set omni to the 400 F for 5 minutes.
4. Serve and enjoy.

Nutritional Value (Amount per Serving):

- Calories 518
- Fat 27.3 g
- Carbohydrates 1.3 g
- Sugar 0.1 g
- Protein 63.9 g
- Cholesterol 204 mg

Quick & Easy Pork Chops

Preparation Time: 10 minutes

Cooking Time: 20 minutes

Serve: 2

Ingredients:

- 2 pork chops, boneless
- 1 tbsp dash seasoning

Directions:

1. Rub seasoning all over the pork chops.
2. Spray cooking pan with cooking spray. Place pork chops on cooking pan.
3. Place cooking pan into the oven and select air fry mode set omni to the 360 F for 20 minutes.
4. Serve and enjoy.

Nutritional Value (Amount per Serving):

- Calories 256
- Fat 19.9 g
- Carbohydrates 0 g
- Sugar 0 g
- Protein 18 g
- Cholesterol 69 mg

Paprika Pork Tenderloin

Preparation Time: 10 minutes

Cooking Time: 30 minutes

Serve: 6

Ingredients:

- 2 lbs pork tenderloin

For rub:

- 1 tbsp smoked paprika
- 1 tbsp garlic powder
- 1 tbsp onion powder
- 1/2 tsp salt

Directions:

1. In a small bowl, combine together all rub ingredients.
2. Coat pork tenderloin with the rub.
3. Heat ovenproof pan over medium-high heat. Spray pan with cooking spray. Sear pork on all sides until lightly golden brown.
4. Select bake mode and set the omni to 425 F for 30 minutes once the oven beeps, place the pan into the oven.
5. Slice and serve.

Nutritional Value (Amount per Serving):

- Calories 228
- Fat 5.5 g
- Carbohydrates 2.6 g
- Sugar 0.9 g
- Protein 40.1 g
- Cholesterol 110 mg

Meatballs

Preparation Time: 10 minutes

Cooking Time: 20 minutes

Serve: 4

Ingredients:

- 1/2 lb ground beef
- 1/2 lb Italian sausage
- 1/2 cup cheddar cheese, shredded
- 1/2 tsp black pepper
- 1/2 tsp garlic powder
- 1/2 tsp onion powder

Directions:

1. Spray air fryer basket with cooking spray.
2. Add all ingredients into the large mixing bowl and mix until well combined.
3. Make small balls from meat mixture and place in the air fryer basket.
4. Place air fryer basket into the oven and select air fry mode set omni to the 370 F for 15 minutes.
5. Turn meatballs and cook for 5 minutes more.
6. Serve and enjoy.

Nutritional Value (Amount per Serving):

- Calories 357
- Fat 24.3 g
- Carbohydrates 0.8 g
- Sugar 0.3 g
- Protein 31.9 g
- Cholesterol 113 mg

Meatloaf

Preparation Time: 10 minutes

Cooking Time: 15 minutes

Serve: 4

Ingredients:

- 2 eggs
- 1 lb ground beef
- 1/4 tsp cinnamon
- 1 tsp cayenne
- 1/2 tsp turmeric
- 1 tsp garam masala
- 1/2 tbsp garlic, minced
- 1/2 tbsp ginger, minced
- 1/4 cup fresh cilantro, chopped
- 1 cup onion, diced
- 1 tsp salt

Directions:

1. Add all ingredients into the mixing bowl and mix until well combined.
2. Transfer meat mixture into the greased loaf pan.
3. Place the loaf pan into the oven and select air fry mode set omni to the 360 F for 15 minutes.
4. Slice and serve.

Nutritional Value (Amount per Serving):

- Calories 261
- Fat 9.5 g
- Carbohydrates 4.3 g
- Sugar 1.5 g
- Protein 37.7 g
- Cholesterol 183 mg

Chapter 7: Seafood Recipes

Tasty Cajun Salmon

Preparation Time: 5 minutes

Cooking Time: 12 minutes

Serve: 2

Ingredients:

- 1 lb salmon fillets
- 1/8 tsp cayenne pepper
- 1 tsp paprika
- 2 tsp onion powder
- 2 tsp garlic powder
- 2 tsp Cajun seasonings
- 3 tbsp olive oil
- 1/4 cup parsley, minced
- 1 lemon juice
- Pepper
- Salt

Directions:

1. In a small bowl, mix together Cajun seasoning, pepper, garlic powder, onion powder, paprika, cayenne pepper, and salt.
2. Brush fillets with oil and rub with spice mixture.
3. Place fish fillets in a baking dish. Pour lemon juice over fish fillets.
4. Select bake mode and set the omni to 450 F for 12 minutes once the oven beeps, place the baking dish into the oven.
5. Garnish with parsley and serve.

Nutritional Value (Amount per Serving):

- Calories 509
- Fat 35.5 g
- Carbohydrates 5.6 g
- Sugar 2.2 g
- Protein 45.3 g
- Cholesterol 100 mg

Delicious Shrimp Scampi

Preparation Time: 5 minutes

Cooking Time: 13 minutes

Serve: 4

Ingredients:

- 1 lb shrimp, peeled and deveined
- 1/4 cup parmesan cheese, grated
- 8 garlic cloves, peeled
- 2 tbsp olive oil
- 1 fresh lemon, cut into wedges

Directions:

1. Preheat the oven to 200 C/ 400 F.
2. Add all ingredients except parmesan cheese into the mixing bowl and toss well.
3. Transfer shrimp mixture into the baking dish.
4. Select bake mode and set the omni to 400 F for 13 minutes once the oven beeps, place the baking dish into the oven.
5. Sprinkle with parmesan cheese and serve.

Nutritional Value (Amount per Serving):

- Calories 228
- Fat 10.3 g
- Carbohydrates 5.3 g
- Sugar 0.4 g
- Protein 28.4 g
- Cholesterol 243 mg

Baked Tilapia

Preparation Time: 5 minutes

Cooking Time: 15 minutes

Serve: 4

Ingredients:

- 1 lb tilapia fillets
- 2 tbsp olive oil
- 2 tbsp dried parsley
- 2 tbsp garlic, minced
- Pepper
- Salt

Directions:

1. Spray cooking pan with cooking spray and set aside.
2. Place fish fillets on cooking pan. Drizzle with oil and season with pepper and salt.
3. Sprinkle garlic and parsley over fish fillets.
4. Select bake mode and set the omni to 400 F for 15 minutes once the oven beeps, place the cooking pan into the oven.
5. Serve and enjoy.

Nutritional Value (Amount per Serving):

- Calories 160
- Fat 8.1 g
- Carbohydrates 1.5 g
- Sugar 0.1 g
- Protein 21.4 g
- Cholesterol 55 mg

Greek Fish

Preparation Time: 5 minutes

Cooking Time: 15 minutes

Serve: 4

Ingredients:

- 4 halibut fish fillets
- 2 tsp olive oil
- 3 tbsp fresh basil, chopped
- 2 tomatoes, chopped
- 2 garlic cloves, minced
- 1 tsp oregano, chopped

Directions:

1. Spray a baking dish with cooking spray and set aside.
2. In a bowl, mix together chopped tomatoes, garlic, oregano, and basil.
3. Arrange fish fillets in a baking dish and top with tomato mixture.
4. Select bake mode and set the omni to 350 F for 15 minutes once the oven beeps, place the baking dish into the oven.
5. Serve and enjoy.

Nutritional Value (Amount per Serving):

- Calories 445
- Fat 22.5 g
- Carbohydrates 35.2 g
- Sugar 1.7 g
- Protein 25.7 g
- Cholesterol 10 mg

Hot Prawns

Preparation Time: 5 minutes

Cooking Time: 8 minutes

Serve: 2

Ingredients:

- 6 prawns
- 1/4 tsp black pepper
- 1/2 tsp chili powder
- 1 tsp chili flakes
- 1/4 tsp salt

Directions:

1. In a bowl, mix together spices add prawns to the bowl and toss well with spices.
2. Spray air fryer basket with cooking spray.
3. Transfer prawns to the air fryer basket.
4. Place air fryer basket into the oven and select air fry mode set omni to the 350 F for 8 minutes.
5. Serve and enjoy.

Nutritional Value (Amount per Serving):

- Calories 81
- Fat 1.2 g
- Carbohydrates 1.6 g
- Sugar 0.1 g
- Protein 15.2 g
- Cholesterol 139 mg

Lemon Garlic Tilapia

Preparation Time: 5 minutes

Cooking Time: 12 minutes

Serve: 4

Ingredients:

- 4 tilapia fillets
- 2 tbsp fresh parsley, chopped
- 1 lemon zest
- 2 tbsp fresh lemon juice
- 3 garlic cloves, minced
- 1/4 cup olive oil
- Pepper
- Salt

Directions:

1. Spray a baking dish with cooking spray and set aside.
2. In a small bowl, whisk together olive oil, lemon zest, lemon juice, and garlic.
3. Season fish fillets with pepper and salt and place onto the baking dish.
4. Pour olive oil mixture over fish fillets.
5. Select bake mode and set the omni to 425 F for 12 minutes once the oven beeps, place the baking dish into the oven.
6. Garnish with parsley and serve.

Nutritional Value (Amount per Serving):

- Calories 211
- Fat 13.8 g
- Carbohydrates 2.4 g
- Sugar 0.6 g
- Protein 21.4 g
- Cholesterol 55 mg

Baked Lemon Cod

Preparation Time: 5 minutes

Cooking Time: 10 minutes

Serve: 2

Ingredients:

- 1 lb cod fillets, rinsed and pat dry
- 1/8 tsp cayenne pepper
- 1 tbsp fresh lemon juice
- 1 tbsp fresh parsley, chopped
- 1 1/2 tbsp olive oil
- 1/4 tsp salt

Directions:

1. Arrange fish fillets on cooking pan. Drizzle with oil and lemon juice and season with cayenne pepper and salt.
2. Select bake mode and set the omni to 400 F for 10 minutes once the oven beeps, place the cooking pan into the oven.
3. Garnish with parsley and serve.

Nutritional Value (Amount per Serving):

- Calories 275
- Fat 11.6 g
- Carbohydrates 0.3 g
- Sugar 0.2 g
- Protein 44.7 g
- Cholesterol 71 mg

Chili Lemon Orange Salmon

Preparation Time: 5 minutes

Cooking Time: 22 minutes

Serve: 4

Ingredients:

- 2 lbs salmon fillet, skinless and boneless
- 1/4 cup fresh dill
- 1 chili, sliced
- 2 fresh lemon juice
- 1 orange juice
- 1 tbsp olive oil
- Pepper
- Salt

Directions:

1. Place salmon fillet in a baking dish and drizzle with olive oil, lemon juice, and orange juice.
2. Sprinkle chili over the salmon and season with pepper and salt.
3. Select bake mode and set the omni to 350 F for 22 minutes once the oven beeps, place the baking dish into the oven.
4. Garnish with dill and serve.

Nutritional Value (Amount per Serving):

- Calories 358
- Fat 18.1 g
- Carbohydrates 4.9 g
- Sugar 2.3 g
- Protein 45.2 g
- Cholesterol 101 mg

Chili Garlic Shrimp

Preparation Time: 5 minutes

Cooking Time: 7

Serve: 4

Ingredients:

- 1 lb shrimp, peeled and deveined
- 1 tbsp olive oil
- 1 lemon, sliced
- 1 red chili, sliced
- 1/2 tsp garlic powder
- Pepper
- Salt

Directions:

1. Spray air fryer basket with cooking spray.
2. Add all ingredients into the mixing bowl and toss well.
3. Transfer shrimp mixture into the air fryer basket.
4. Place air fryer basket into the oven and select air fry mode set omni to the 400 F for 7 minutes. Stir halfway through.
5. Serve and enjoy.

Nutritional Value (Amount per Serving):

- Calories 171
- Fat 5.5 g
- Carbohydrates 3.4 g
- Sugar 0.5 g
- Protein 26.1 g
- Cholesterol 239 mg

Easy Ginger Garlic Shrimp

Preparation Time: 5 minutes

Cooking Time: 20 minutes

Serve: 4

Ingredients:

- 2 eggs
- 1 lb shrimp, peeled and deveined
- 1 tsp garlic powder
- 1 tsp ginger
- 1/2 cup almond flour
- 1 tsp black pepper

Directions:

1. Whisk eggs in a bowl with pepper, garlic powder, and ginger.
2. Add almond flour in a shallow dish.
3. Spray air fryer basket with cooking spray.
4. Dip shrimp in egg mixture then coat with almond flour. Place shrimp into the air fryer basket.
5. Place air fryer basket into the oven and select air fry mode set omni to the 350 F for 20 minutes. Stir halfway through.
6. Serve and enjoy.

Nutritional Value (Amount per Serving):

- Calories 191
- Fat 5.9 g
- Carbohydrates 3.8 g
- Sugar 0.5 g
- Protein 29.6 g
- Cholesterol 321 mg

Chapter 8: Snacks & Appetizers

Buffalo Chicken Dip

Preparation Time: 10 minutes

Cooking Time: 10 minutes

Serve: 8

Ingredients:

- 2 can chunk chicken, drained
- 2 cups cheddar cheese, shredded
- 1 cup ranch dressing
- 1 package cream cheese
- 3/4 cup hot sauce

Directions:

1. Add chicken and hot sauce to the pan and cook for 2 minutes.
2. Add cream and ranch dressing and stir well.
3. Add half cheese and stir until well blended.
4. Transfer chicken mixture to the baking dish and sprinkle the remaining cheese on top.
5. Select bake mode and set the omni to 370 F for 10 minutes once the oven beeps, place the baking dish into the oven.
6. Serve and enjoy.

Nutritional Value (Amount per Serving):

- Calories 514
- Fat 18 g
- Carbohydrates 4 g
- Sugar 2 g
- Protein 24 g
- Cholesterol 113 mg

Cheese Stuffed Jalapenos

Preparation Time: 10 minutes

Cooking Time: 25 minutes

Serve: 4

Ingredients:

- 10 jalapeno peppers, halved, remove seeds & membranes
- 1 tsp onion powder
- 1 tsp garlic powder
- 1 oz cheddar cheese, shredded
- 6 oz cream cheese

Directions:

1. Spray cooking pan with cooking spray and set aside.
2. In a small bowl, mix together cream cheese, garlic powder, and onion powder.
3. Stuff cream cheese mixture into each jalapeno halves.
4. Place jalapeno halves onto the prepared cooking pan and top with shredded cheddar cheese.
5. Select bake mode and set the omni to 350 F for 25 minutes once the oven beeps, place the cooking pan into the oven.
6. Serve and enjoy.

Nutritional Value (Amount per Serving):

- Calories 196
- Fat 17.7 g
- Carbohydrates 4.8 g
- Sugar 1.7 g
- Protein 5.7 g
- Cholesterol 54 mg

Parmesan Potatoes

Preparation Time: 10 minutes

Cooking Time: 45 minutes

Serve: 2

Ingredients:

- 5 medium potatoes, peeled and cut into 1/2-inch pieces
- 3 tbsp olive oil
- 1 tsp garlic powder
- 1 tsp paprika
- 1/2 cup parmesan cheese, grated
- Salt

Directions:

1. Line cooking pan with parchment paper and set aside.
2. In a mixing bowl, add potatoes and remaining ingredients and toss to coat.
3. Arrange potatoes on a prepared cooking pan.
4. Select bake mode and set the omni to 450 F for 30 minutes once the oven beeps, place the cooking pan into the oven.
5. Turn potatoes and bake for 10-15 minutes more.
6. Serve and enjoy.

Nutritional Value (Amount per Serving):

- Calories 635
- Fat 27 g
- Carbohydrates 86.2 g
- Sugar 6.6 g
- Protein 17.4 g
- Cholesterol 18 mg

Easy Baked Potato Wedges

Preparation Time: 10 minutes

Cooking Time: 30 minutes

Serve: 4

Ingredients:

- 2 large potatoes, cut into wedges
- 2 tbsp olive oil
- 1 tbsp ranch seasoning

Directions:

1. Line cooking pan with parchment paper and set aside.
2. Add potato wedges, oil, and ranch seasoning in mixing bowl and toss well.
3. Arrange potato wedges onto the prepared cooking pan.
4. Select bake mode and set the omni to 400 F for 15 minutes once the oven beeps, place the cooking pan into the oven.
5. Turn potato wedges and bake for 15 minutes more.
6. Serve and enjoy.

Nutritional Value (Amount per Serving):

- Calories 195
- Fat 7.2 g
- Carbohydrates 29 g
- Sugar 2.1 g
- Protein 3.1 g
- Cholesterol 0 mg

Air Fried Cauliflower Florets

Preparation Time: 10 minutes

Cooking Time: 15 minutes

Serve: 4

Ingredients:

- 1 medium cauliflower head, cut into florets
- 1/2 tsp old bay seasoning
- 1/4 tsp paprika
- 1 tbsp garlic, minced
- 3 tbsp olive oil
- Pepper
- Salt

Directions:

1. In a large bowl, toss cauliflower with remaining ingredients.
2. Spread cauliflower florets onto the cooking pan.
3. Place cooking pan into the oven and select air fry mode set omni to the 400 F for 15 minutes. Stir twice.
4. Serve and enjoy.

Nutritional Value (Amount per Serving):

- Calories 130
- Fat 10.7 g
- Carbohydrates 8.4 g
- Sugar 3.5 g
- Protein 3 g
- Cholesterol 0 mg

Cauliflower Hummus

Preparation Time: 10 minutes

Cooking Time: 35 minutes

Serve: 8

Ingredients:

- 1 cauliflower head, cut into florets
- 3 tbsp olive oil
- 1/2 tsp ground cumin
- 1 tsp garlic, chopped
- 2 tbsp fresh lemon juice
- 1/3 cup tahini
- Pepper
- Salt

Directions:

1. Spray cooking pan with cooking spray.
2. Spread cauliflower florets onto the prepared cooking pan.
3. Select bake mode and set the omni to 400 F for 35 minutes once the oven beeps, place the cooking pan into the oven. Turn cauliflower florets halfway through.
4. Transfer cauliflower florets into the food processor along with remaining ingredients and process until smooth.
5. Serve and enjoy.

Nutritional Value (Amount per Serving):

- Calories 115
- Fat 10.7 g
- Carbohydrates 4.2 g
- Sugar 0.9 g
- Protein 2.4 g
- Cholesterol 0 mg

Easy Roasted Brussels Sprouts

Preparation Time: 10 minutes

Cooking Time: 35 minutes

Serve: 6

Ingredients:

- 2 cups Brussels sprouts, halved
- 1/4 tsp garlic powder
- 1/4 cup olive oil
- 1/4 tsp cayenne pepper
- 1/4 tsp salt

Directions:

1. Add all ingredients into the large bowl and toss well.
2. Transfer Brussels sprouts on a cooking pan.
3. Select bake mode and set the omni to 400 F for 35 minutes once the oven beeps, place the cooking pan into the oven. Turn halfway through.
4. Serve and enjoy.

Nutritional Value (Amount per Serving):

- Calories 85
- Fat 8.5 g
- Carbohydrates 2.8 g
- Sugar 0.7 g
- Protein 1 g
- Cholesterol 0 mg

Sweet Potato Croquettes

Preparation Time: 10 minutes

Cooking Time: 60 minutes

Serve: 6

Ingredients:

- 2 cups cooked quinoa
- 2 tsp Italian seasoning
- 2 cups sweet potatoes, mashed
- 1/4 cup scallions, chopped
- 1/4 cup parsley, chopped
- 1/4 cup flour
- 1 garlic clove, minced
- 1/4 cup celery, diced
- Pepper
- Salt

Directions:

1. Spray cooking pan with cooking spray and set aside.
2. Add all ingredients into the large bowl and mix until well combined.
3. Make 1-inch round croquettes from mixture and place on a prepared cooking pan.
4. Select bake mode and set the omni to 375 F for 60 minutes once the oven beeps, place the cooking pan into the oven.
5. Serve and enjoy.

Nutritional Value (Amount per Serving):

- Calories 295
- Fat 4.1 g
- Carbohydrates 55.2 g
- Sugar 0.6 g
- Protein 9.5 g
- Cholesterol 1 mg

Cheese Dip

Preparation Time: 10 minutes

Cooking Time: 10 minutes

Serve: 4

Ingredients:

- 10 oz goat cheese
- 2 tbsp olive oil
- 1/4 cup parmesan cheese
- 2 garlic cloves, minced
- 1/4 tsp sage
- 1/4 tsp thyme
- Pepper
- Salt

Directions:

1. Spray a baking dish with cooking spray and set aside.
2. Add all ingredients into the food processor and process until just combined.
3. Pour mixture into the prepared baking dish and spread well.
4. Select bake mode and set the omni to 400 F for 10 minutes once the oven beeps, place the baking dish into the oven.
5. Serve and enjoy.

Nutritional Value (Amount per Serving):

- Calories 403
- Fat 33.6 g
- Carbohydrates 2.3 g
- Sugar 1.6 g
- Protein 23.8 g
- Cholesterol 79 mg

Herb Mushrooms

Preparation Time: 10 minutes

Cooking Time: 14 minutes

Serve: 4

Ingredients:

- 1 lb mushrooms
- 1/2 tsp ground coriander
- 1 tsp rosemary, chopped
- 1 tbsp basil, minced
- 1 garlic clove, minced
- 1/2 tbsp vinegar
- Pepper
- Salt

Directions:

1. Add all ingredients into the large bowl and toss well.
2. Spread mushrooms onto the cooking pan.
3. Place cooking pan into the oven and select air fry mode set omni to the 350 F for 14 minutes. Stir halfway through.
4. Serve and enjoy.

Nutritional Value (Amount per Serving):

- Calories 27
- Fat 0.4 g
- Carbohydrates 4.2 g
- Sugar 2 g
- Protein 3.6 g
- Cholesterol 0 mg

Chapter 9: Dehydrated Recipes

Spicy Kale Chips

Preparation Time: 10 minutes

Cooking Time: 11 hours

Serve: 4 cups

Ingredients:

- 5 oz fresh kale leaves

For sauce:

- 1 chipotle pepper
- 2 tbsp lemon juice
- 1 cup of water
- 1/2 cup sunflower seeds
- 1 cup cashews
- 1/4 tsp salt

Directions:

1. Add all sauce ingredients into the blender and blend until smooth.
2. Add kale leaves into the mixing bowl. Pour sauce over kale leaves mix until kale leaves are well coated with sauce.
3. Line cooking pan with parchment paper.
4. Arrange kale leaves on the cooking pan in a single layer.
5. Place cooking pan in an Instant Omni Air Fryer Oven Combo. Select dehydrate mode and set the omni to 155 F for 1 hour.
6. Turn temperature to 115 F and set a timer for 10 hours.
7. Serve and enjoy.

Nutritional Value (Amount per Serving):

- Calories 254
- Fat 18.9 g
- Carbohydrates 17.3 g
- Sugar 2.6 g
- Protein 7.8 g
- Cholesterol 0 mg

Kiwi Chips

Preparation Time: 5 minutes

Cooking Time: 10 hours

Serve: 4

Ingredients:

- 6 kiwis, wash and pat dry well

Directions:

1. Peel kiwis and cut into 1/4-inch thick slices.
2. Arrange kiwi slices on the cooking pan in a single layer.
3. Place cooking pan in an Instant Omni Air Fryer Oven Combo. Select dehydrate mode and set the omni to 135 F for 10 hours.
4. Serve and enjoy.

Nutritional Value (Amount per Serving):

- Calories 70
- Fat 0.6 g
- Carbohydrates 16.7 g
- Sugar 10.3 g
- Protein 1.3 g
- Cholesterol 0 mg

Beef Jerky

Preparation Time: 10 minutes

Cooking Time: 8 hours

Serve: 6

Ingredients:

- 1 lb flank steak, cut into thin slices
- 1 1/2 tbsp ranch seasoning
- 1/2 cup Worcestershire sauce
- 1/2 cup soy sauce
- 1/8 tsp cayenne pepper
- 3/4 tsp liquid smoke
- 1 tbsp red pepper flakes

Directions:

1. Add all ingredients into the large zip-lock bag. Seal bag and mix well and place in refrigerator overnight.
2. Arrange marinated meat slices on a cooking pan in a single layer.
3. Place cooking pan in an Instant Omni Air Fryer Oven Combo. Select dehydrate mode and set the omni to 145 F for 8 hours.

Nutritional Value (Amount per Serving):

- Calories 186
- Fat 6.3 g
- Carbohydrates 5.6 g
- Sugar 4.4 g
- Protein 22.4 g
- Cholesterol 42 mg

Squash Chips

Preparation Time: 5 minutes

Cooking Time: 12 hours

Serve: 8

Ingredients:

- 2 cups yellow squash, sliced 1/8-inch thick
- 2 tbsp apple cider vinegar
- 2 tsp olive oil
- Salt

Directions:

1. In a mixing bowl, mix squash slices, vinegar, oil, and salt.
2. Arrange squash slices on cooking pan in a single layer.
3. Place cooking pan in an Instant Omni Air Fryer Oven Combo. Select dehydrate mode and set the omni to 110 F for 12 hours.
4. Serve and enjoy.

Nutritional Value (Amount per Serving):

- Calories 15
- Fat 1.2 g
- Carbohydrates 1 g
- Sugar 0.5 g
- Protein 0.3 g
- Cholesterol 0 mg

Easy Chicken Jerky

Preparation Time: 10 minutes

Cooking Time: 7 hours

Serve: 4

Ingredients:

- 1 lb chicken tenders, boneless, skinless and cut into 1/4-inch slices
- 1/2 tsp garlic powder
- 1 tsp lemon juice
- 1/2 cup soy sauce
- 1/4 tsp ground ginger
- 1/4 tsp black pepper

Directions:

1. Mix all ingredients except chicken slices into the zip-lock bag.
2. Add chicken and seal bag and mix well. Place the bag in the refrigerator for 30 minutes.
3. Arrange chicken slices on cooking pan in a single layer.
4. Place cooking pan in an Instant Omni Air Fryer Oven Combo. Select dehydrate mode and set the omni to 145 F for 7 hours.

Nutritional Value (Amount per Serving):

- Calories 235
- Fat 8.4 g
- Carbohydrates 2.9 g
- Sugar 0.7 g
- Protein 34.9 g
- Cholesterol 101 mg

Dehydrated Banana Slices

Preparation Time: 10 minutes

Cooking Time: 8 hours

Serve: 4

Ingredients:

- 2 bananas, cut into 1/8-inch thick slices
- 1/2 cup fresh lemon juice

Directions:

1. Add sliced bananas and lemon juice in a mixing bowl and mix well.
2. Arrange sliced bananas on cooking pan in a single layer
3. Place cooking pan in an Instant Omni Air Fryer Oven Combo. Select dehydrate mode and set the omni to 135 F for 8 hours.

Nutritional Value (Amount per Serving):

- Calories 60
- Fat 0.4 g
- Carbohydrates 14.1 g
- Sugar 7.9 g
- Protein 0.9 g
- Cholesterol 0 mg

Balsamic Zucchini Chips

Preparation Time: 10 minutes

Cooking Time: 12 hours

Serve: 8

Ingredients:

- 4 cups zucchini, cut into thin slices
- 2 tbsp olive oil
- 2 tbsp balsamic vinegar
- 2 tsp sea salt

Directions:

1. Add olive oil, balsamic vinegar, and sea salt to the large bowl and stir well.
2. Add sliced zucchini to the bowl and toss well.
3. Arrange zucchini slices on the cooking pan in a single layer.
4. Place cooking pan in an Instant Omni Air Fryer Oven Combo. Select dehydrate mode and set the omni to 135 F for 12 hours.

Nutritional Value (Amount per Serving):

- Calories 40
- Fat 3.6 g
- Carbohydrates 1.9 g
- Sugar 1 g
- Protein 0.7 g
- Cholesterol 0 mg

Simple Kale Chips

Preparation Time: 10 minutes

Cooking Time: 4 hours

Serve: 4

Ingredients:

- 2 kale heads, wash and cut into bits
- 1 tbsp fresh lemon juice
- 3 tbsp nutritional yeast
- 2 tbsp olive oil
- 1 tsp garlic powder
- 1 tsp sea salt

Directions:

1. Add kale and remaining ingredients into the bowl and mix until well coated.
2. Arrange kale bits on cooking pan in a single layer.
3. Place cooking pan in an Instant Omni Air Fryer Oven Combo. Select dehydrate mode and set the omni to 145 F for 4 hours.

Nutritional Value (Amount per Serving):

- Calories 111
- Fat 7.5 g
- Carbohydrates 8.5 g
- Sugar 0.3 g
- Protein 4.9 g
- Cholesterol 0 mg

Flavorful Almonds

Preparation Time: 10 minutes

Cooking Time: 24 hours

Serve: 6

Ingredients:

- 2 cups almonds, soak in water for overnight
- 1 tbsp fresh rosemary, chopped
- 1 tsp chili powder
- 1 tbsp olive oil
- 3/4 tsp kosher salt

Directions:

1. Add all ingredients into the mixing bowl and mix well.
2. Arrange almonds on cooking pan.
3. Place cooking pan in an Instant Omni Air Fryer Oven Combo. Select dehydrate mode and set the omni to 125 F for 24 hours.

Nutritional Value (Amount per Serving):

- Calories 206
- Fat 18.3 g
- Carbohydrates 7.4 g
- Sugar 1.4 g
- Protein 6.8 g
- Cholesterol 0 mg

Dehydrated Bell Peppers

Preparation Time: 10 minutes

Cooking Time: 24 hours

Serve: 4

Ingredients:

- 4 bell peppers, cut in half and remove seeds

Directions:

1. Cut bell peppers in strips then cut each strip in 1/2-inch pieces.
2. Arrange bell pepper strips on cooking pan in a single layer.
3. Place cooking pan in an Instant Omni Air Fryer Oven Combo. Select dehydrate mode and set the omni to 135 F for 24 hours.

Nutritional Value (Amount per Serving):

- Calories 38
- Fat 0.3 g
- Carbohydrates 9 g
- Sugar 6 g
- Protein 1.2 g
- Cholesterol 0 mg

Chapter 10: Desserts

Moist French Yogurt Cake

Preparation Time: 10 minutes

Cooking Time: 35 minutes

Serve: 12

Ingredients:

- 2 eggs
- 4 tbsp oil
- 7 oz sugar
- 7 oz all-purpose flour
- 2 tsp baking powder
- 8.5 oz yogurt

Directions:

1. In a large bowl, add yogurt, oil, eggs, sugar, flour, and baking powder and mix until smooth.
2. Pour batter into the greased cake pan.
3. Select bake mode and set the toaster oven to 350 F for 35 minutes once the oven beeps, place the cake pan into the oven.
4. Slice and serve.

Nutritional Value (Amount per Serving):

- Calories 188
- Fat 5.7 g
- Carbohydrates 31 g
- Sugar 18.1 g
- Protein 3.8 g
- Cholesterol 28 mg

Lemon Muffins

Preparation Time: 10 minutes

Cooking Time: 20 minutes

Serve: 12

Ingredients:

- 1 egg
- 1 cup ricotta cheese
- 1 tsp lemon extract
- 1 tbsp fresh lemon juice
- 1 tbsp lemon zest, grated
- 1/2 cup butter, softened
- 1 cup of sugar
- 1/2 tsp baking soda
- 1/2 tsp baking powder
- 2 cups flour
- 1/2 tsp salt

Directions:

1. Line muffin tray with cupcake liners and set aside.
2. In a mixing bowl, mix together egg, sugar, and butter.
3. Add lemon extract, lemon juice, lemon zest, and ricotta cheese and mix well.
4. In a separate bowl, mix together flour, baking soda, baking powder, and salt.
5. Add flour mixture into the egg mixture and mix until well combined.
6. Pour batter into the prepared muffin tray.
7. Select bake mode and set the omni to 350 F for 20 minutes once the oven beeps, place muffin tray into the oven.
8. Serve and enjoy.

Nutritional Value (Amount per Serving):

- Calories 242
- Fat 9.9 g
- Carbohydrates 33.9 g
- Sugar 16.9 g
- Protein 5.1 g
- Cholesterol 40 mg

Carrot Cake

Preparation Time: 10 minutes

Cooking Time: 25 minutes

Serve: 18

Ingredients:

- 2 eggs, lightly beaten
- 1 tsp vanilla
- 1/2 cup vegetable oil
- 1/4 cup white sugar
- 3/4 cup brown sugar
- 2 1/2 cups shredded carrots
- 1 1/4 tsp cinnamon
- 1/4 tsp baking soda
- 1 tsp baking powder
- 1 1/2 cups all-purpose flour

Directions:

1. Grease 9*13-inch cake pan and set aside.
2. In a large bowl, mix flour, cinnamon, baking soda, and baking powder.
3. In a separate bowl, whisk eggs, shredded carrots, white sugar, brown sugar, vanilla, and oil.
4. Add egg mixture into the flour mixture and mix until just combined.
5. Pour batter into the prepared cake pan and spread evenly.
6. Select bake mode and set the toaster oven to 350 F for 25 minutes once the oven beeps, place the cake pan into the oven.
7. Slice and serve.

Nutritional Value (Amount per Serving):

- Calories 139
- Fat 6.7 g
- Carbohydrates 18.5 g
- Sugar 9.5 g
- Protein 1.9 g
- Cholesterol 18 mg

Moist & Light Chocolate Cake

Preparation Time: 10 minutes

Cooking Time: 40 minutes

Serve: 18

Ingredients:

- 3 cups flour
- 2 cups cold water
- 2 tbsp white vinegar
- 2 tsp vanilla
- 10 tbsp oil
- 2 tsp baking soda
- 5 tbsp cocoa powder
- 2 cups of sugar
- 1 tsp salt

Directions:

1. Add all ingredients into the mixing bowl and mix until well combined.
2. Pour batter into the 9*13-inch cake pan.
3. Select bake mode and set the toaster oven to 350 F for 40 minutes once the oven beeps, place the cake pan into the oven.
4. Top with fresh whipped cream.
5. Slice and serve.

Nutritional Value (Amount per Serving):

- Calories 231
- Fat 8 g
- Carbohydrates 39 g
- Sugar 22.4 g
- Protein 2.4 g
- Cholesterol 0 mg

Blueberry Muffins

Preparation Time: 10 minutes

Cooking Time: 30 minutes

Serve: 12

Ingredients:

- 2 eggs
- 2 1/2 cups blueberries
- 2 tsp baking powder
- 3/4 cup sugar
- 2 cups all-purpose flour
- 1/2 cup milk
- 8 tbsp butter, melted
- 1 tsp kosher salt

Directions:

1. Line muffin tray with cupcake liners and set aside.
2. In a mixing bowl, whisk together eggs, butter, and milk.
3. In a large bowl, mix together flour, baking powder, sugar, and salt.
4. Add egg mixture into the flour mixture and mix until well combined.
5. Add blueberries and fold well. Pour batter into the prepared muffin tray.
6. Select bake mode and set the omni to 375 F for 30 minutes once the oven beeps, place muffin tray into the oven.
7. Serve and enjoy.

Nutritional Value (Amount per Serving):

- Calories 224
- Fat 8.9 g
- Carbohydrates 33.7 g
- Sugar 16.1 g
- Protein 3.7 g
- Cholesterol 48 mg

Strawberry Cobbler

Preparation Time: 10 minutes

Cooking Time: 45 minutes

Serve: 6

Ingredients:

- 2 cups strawberries, diced
- 1 tsp vanilla
- 1 cup self-rising flour
- 1 1/4 cup sugar
- 1/2 cup butter, melted
- 1 cup unsweetened almond milk

Directions:

1. Grease 11*8-inch baking dish and set aside.
2. In a bowl, mix together flour and 1 cup sugar.
3. Add milk and whisk until smooth.
4. Add vanilla and butter and mix well.
5. Pour mixture into the prepared baking dish and sprinkle with strawberries and top with remaining sugar.
6. Select bake mode and set the omni to 350 F for 45 minutes once the oven beeps, place the baking dish into the oven.
7. Serve and enjoy.

Nutritional Value (Amount per Serving):

- Calories 392
- Fat 16.3 g
- Carbohydrates 61.7 g
- Sugar 44.2 g
- Protein 2.8 g
- Cholesterol 41 mg

Almond Butter Banana Brownies

Preparation Time: 10 minutes

Cooking Time: 20 minutes

Serve: 4

Ingredients:

- 1 scoop protein powder
- 2 tbsp cocoa powder
- 1/2 cup almond butter
- 1 cup bananas

Directions:

1. Spray baking dish with cooking spray.
2. Add all ingredients into the blender and blend until smooth.
3. Pour batter into the prepared baking dish.
4. Select bake mode and set the omni to 350 F for 20 minutes once the oven beeps, place the baking dish into the oven.
5. Serve and enjoy.

Nutritional Value (Amount per Serving):

- Calories 82
- Fat 2.1 g
- Carbohydrates 11.4 g
- Sugar 5 g
- Protein 6.9 g
- Cholesterol 16 mg

Delicious Strawberry Bars

Preparation Time: 10 minutes

Cooking Time: 30 minutes

Serve: 16

Ingredients:

- 3/4 cup strawberry preserves
- 1 tsp xanthan gum
- 3/4 cup brown sugar
- 1 cup rolled oats
- 1 cup flour, gluten-free
- 1 tsp vanilla
- 10 tbsp butter, melted
- 1 tsp baking soda
- 1/4 tsp salt

Directions:

1. Grease 8*8 baking dish and set aside.
2. In a large bowl, whisk together flour, baking soda, xanthan gum, brown sugar, rolled oats, and salt.
3. Add melted butter and vanilla in flour mixture and stir to combine.
4. Set aside 1/3 of the flour mixture. Transfer the remaining mixture to the prepared baking dish and press down with a spatula.
5. Spread strawberry preserves on top.
6. Spread remaining flour mixture over the strawberry layer.
7. Select bake mode and set the omni to 350 F for 30 minutes once the oven beeps, place the baking dish into the oven.
8. Slice and serve.

Nutritional Value (Amount per Serving):

- Calories 180
- Fat 7.6 g
- Carbohydrates 26.7 g
- Sugar 14 g
- Protein 1.7 g
- Cholesterol 19 mg

Pumpkin Muffins

Preparation Time: 10 minutes

Cooking Time: 35 minutes

Serve: 12

Ingredients:

- 2 eggs
- 1/2 cup maple syrup
- 1 tsp pumpkin pie spice
- 1 tsp baking soda
- 2 cups all-purpose flour
- 1/2 cup chocolate chips
- 1 cup can pumpkin
- 1/2 cup olive oil
- 1/2 tsp salt

Directions:

1. Line muffin tray with cupcake liners and set aside.
2. In a large bowl, mix together flour, pumpkin pie spice, baking soda, and salt.
3. In a separate bowl, whisk together eggs, pumpkin puree, oil, and maple syrup.
4. Slowly add dry mixture to the wet mixture and mix well. Add chocolate chips and fold well.
5. Pour batter into the prepared muffin tray.
6. Select bake mode and set the omni to 350 F for 35 minutes once the oven beeps, place muffin tray into the oven.
7. Serve and enjoy.

Nutritional Value (Amount per Serving):

- Calories 237
- Fat 11.5 g
- Carbohydrates 30.7 g
- Sugar 12.2 g
- Protein 3.8 g
- Cholesterol 29 mg

Delicious Peanut Butter Cake

Preparation Time: 10 minutes

Cooking Time: 30 minutes

Serve: 8

Ingredients:

- 1 1/2 cups all-purpose flour
- 1/2 cup peanut butter powder
- 1 cup of sugar
- 1 tsp vanilla
- 1 tbsp apple cider vinegar
- 1 cup of water
- 1/3 cup vegetable oil
- 1 tsp baking soda
- 1/2 tsp salt

Directions:

1. Spray cake pan with cooking spray and set aside.
2. In a large mixing bowl, mix together flour, baking soda, peanut butter powder, sugar, and salt.
3. In a small bowl, whisk together oil, vanilla, vinegar, and water.
4. Pour oil mixture into the flour mixture and stir to combine.
5. Pour batter into the prepared pan.
6. Select bake mode and set the omni to 350 F for 30 minutes once the oven beeps, place the cake pan into the oven.
7. Slice and enjoy.

Nutritional Value (Amount per Serving):

- Calories 264
- Fat 9.4 g
- Carbohydrates 43.2 g
- Sugar 25.3 g
- Protein 2.6 g
- Cholesterol 0 mg

Conclusion

If you have such a functional oven and you are willing to lose belly fat without stopping eating tasty food, Cooking the perfect keto diet without sacrificing the taste can be a really hard process. There are many steps you need to master and take into account. But with high-quality recipes and proper instructions, you will enjoy yourself.

Now you can save time, money, and start eating healthier versions of your favorite foods using your machine's full power, thanks to this revolutionary cookbook! Stop wasting your time trying to find delicious and healthy recipes. Grab a copy of this cookbook and start enjoying the crunch without the calories and messy cleanup with Keto Instant Omni Pro Air Fryer Oven Combo Cookbook!

CPSIA information can be obtained
at www.ICGtesting.com
Printed in the USA
LVHW020926191221
706632LV00004B/507

9 781915 038395